MOLLY

A Play

SIMON GRAY

SAMUEL FRENCH

LONDON
NEW YORK SYDNEY TORONTO HOLLYWOOD

FOR AMATEUR PRODUCTION ENQUIRIES

UNITED KINGDOM AND WORLD
EXCLUDING NORTH AMERICA
plays@samuelfrench.co.uk
020 7255 4302/01

Each title is subject to availability from Samuel French,
depending upon country of performance.

MOLLY

The British Premiere of the play was presented at the Palace Theatre, Watford in November 1977. Subsequently presented by H. M. Tennent Ltd, in association with Grosvenor Entertainments and Shineline Ltd, at the Comedy Theatre on 25th October 1978, with the following cast of characters:

Molly	Billie Whitelaw
Teddy	T. P. McKenna
Eve	Barbara Atkinson
Oliver	Anthony Allen
Greaves	Michael Shannon
Police Constable	David Telfer

The play directed by Stephen Hollis

Setting by Christopher Morley

The action takes place in the living-room of Molly's and Teddy's house

Act I   Scene 1 Late afternoon
            Scene 2 A week or so later—mid-afternoon
            Scene 3 About one hour later
Act II   Scene 1 A week or so later—mid-afternoon
            Scene 2 Two hours later
            Scene 3 About one hour later
            Scene 4 Some months later—afternoon

Time—the 1930s

ACT I

Scene 1

The living-room of a house. Late afternoon, the nineteen-thirties

The room has three doors: one to the conservatory, part of which is visible on the stage; one to the hall, stairs and front door; one to a corridor to the kitchen, dining-room, etc. In the room is a drinks trolley, new and of the nineteen-thirties, amply stocked, a piano, large sofa, armchairs, tables, all in the style of the nineteen-thirties

When the Curtain *rises the room is empty. After a moment Molly, wearing a light coat and silk scarf, enters from the conservatory, smoking. She goes to the sofa, sits and muses. She looks across at the drinks trolley, rises and goes to it, pours a neat gin, knocks it back and pours another*

Teddy (*calling from upstairs*) Moll! Moll! Moll!

A door slams upstairs and footsteps are heard coming down

> *Molly puts her glass down and exits quickly through the conservatory. Teddy enters, calling "Moll" irritably. He goes to the corridor door and calls, then to the conservatory. Teddy is in his mid-sixties, and has a deaf-aid—elaborate and visible, of the nineteen-thirties style. He has an air of slightly bogus physicality.*

> *Eve enters from the corridor, wearing a pair of oven gloves. She is a woman in her mid-fifties, severely dressed and severe of expression: spectacles, an air of brisk efficiency*

Teddy (*off*) Damn it! (*He comes back from the conservatory, sees Eve?* Oh, hello Evie, where's Moll?

Eve (*speaking loudly*) She's gone for a walk.

Teddy When?

Eve About an hour ago.

Teddy Then why didn't she ask me. I could have just done with a walk.

Eve You were taking a nap.

Teddy But I didn't want to. I wanted to go for a walk. (*He goes to the drinks trolley*) I spend the whole afternoon waiting for her to make up her mind whether she wants to go or not—(*pouring himself a Scotch*)—and when I go upstairs to get a book and sit down on the bed with it for a moment and . . . (*He adds soda water to his Scotch, splashes it*) Damn, damn!

Eve I'll get a cloth . . .

Teddy Oh sit down Evie, sit down. I can manage. (*He mops up the soda with a handkerchief*) Sorry, Eve, I'm always a grump if I doze through the afternoon—like a bear with a headache—what'll you have, one of your dry as dust sherrys?

Eve Oh, no thank you, Teddy, I really ought to get back to the kitchen . . . (*She sits as Teddy speaks*)

Teddy (*pouring Eve a sherry*) Tell me, Evie, do you think Moll wants to stay. We've been here a month now but she makes me feel as if we only just moved in yesterday, or we're going to be moved out tomorrow, but we're never going to have the part in between, has she said anything to you? (*He brings her the sherry*)

Eve Thank you. Well, she's said she likes it here.

Teddy What about you?

Eve Oh yes. Very much.

Teddy That's good, because, we need you, Evie. Your hitching on to us was real luck, you keep us orderly. Don't you think of abandoning us.

Eve That's very kind of you, Teddy.

Teddy (*sitting on the sofa*) Well, it's her England, that's what she said she wanted. And it'd do for me if she settles for it. Wish I didn't sleep so much, that's the only thing. Never slept like this in Canada. Never had time to. But then I had a business to run, bills of lading to get out, had to meet the ships at sometimes two in the morning, did you know that, Evie? (*Pause*) Funny thing is I miss the smell of fish. The whole town smelt of it, the uptown streets, it got into the stores. I didn't notice it until I'd left. Hey, it's getting dark. That's something else I'm not used to, your English springs. We don't have springs in Canada, just a sort of wink between winter and summer. But then we have our falls, you don't have falls, do you?

Eve No, we only have autumns, I'm afraid.

Teddy What? Well, I don't like her out in the dark. Wandering about. She used to tell me England's got the best climate in the world, you know what I think now I've seen it, it may be the best climate, but the weather's terrible. (*He laughs*) Not my idea of friendly either. (*He rises and goes back to the drinks trolley*) Now in Nova Scotia, move into a village they'd be right round asking what they could do to help, inviting us over, but we've been here two whole weeks, and who do we know, Dr Gracey, when I need him to look after my ears.

Eve More people know Tom Fool than Tom Fool knows people.

Teddy Who? (*He pours himself another drink*)

Eve Tom Fool.

Teddy Tom who?

Eve Fool.

Teddy Well I don't know him, somebody in the village?

Eve It's a saying.

Teddy (*not having understood*) Oh. Ready for another? (*He comes across with the bottle*)

Eve No I won't, thanks . . .

Teddy pours sherry. Eve just manages to catch it in her glass

Teddy You know what woke me up? (*Replacing the bottle*) I thought I heard her singing, that one about the seals of Nanaimo, and playing the piano—I heard it quite clear, every note, so it must have been a dream—

she was going to try and write more songs once she got back here, that's why she wanted a place with a piano in it, but she hasn't played it yet—I'm going to get on to her about that, this evening. Did you know I got that seal song played over Station RCVX—knew the owner—he put it out across the whole of Nova Scotia. Bob Hoskins. He was a good friend of mine. In hardware. You ever been married, Evie?
Eve No.
Teddy Why not?
Eve I'm afraid no-one ever asked me.
Teddy That's the girl. (*He laughs*) Hey, Evie, mind if I ask you a delicate question?
Eve No.
Teddy You sure?
Eve Well, as I'm living in your house, you have a perfect right to know anything about me you want. Within reason, of course.
Teddy Am I paying you enough? (*He makes to refill her glass*)
Eve Yes, quite enough, thank you, Teddy. (*Refusing more drink*) No thank you. You're more than generous. Now if you'll excuse me I really must go and have a look at the dinner. (*She rises*)

Eve exits to the corridor

Teddy Oh. (*He sits for a moment, then gets up, goes to the drinks trolley, adds a dash of Scotch, squirts soda water, splashes it slightly, makes as if to mop it, gestures irritably, goes over to the conservatory, stands looking through*) What the hell's she playing at?

There is a ring at the door-bell. Teddy makes no move

Eve appears in the doorway

Eve Somebody at the door.

Teddy still makes no move

Eve makes to speak, then goes out to the hall

Teddy (*moving to the door to the corridor*) Hey Evie, I'm getting really worried . . .

Eve enters from the hall, accompanied by Oliver. Oliver is a boy of about seventeen, awkward and not particularly attractive: dressed in his Sunday clothes, as for an interview

Teddy turns away from the door, sees Oliver and Eve

Eve (*coming over to Teddy*) It's a boy from the village.
Teddy What? Is Moll all right?
Eve He says something about a job.
Teddy What job?
Eve I've no idea.
Teddy (*going over to Oliver*) Well hello, boy, what can we do for you?
Oliver Sir. They said at Sprinkley's there was a job.

Eve That's the garage in the village.

Teddy What's your name, boy?

Oliver Oliver, sir.

Teddy What?

Oliver Oliver, sir. Oliver Treefe.

Teddy Oliver?

Oliver Yes, sir.

Teddy Oliver what, Oliver?

Oliver Oliver Treefe, sir.

Eve You'll have to speak up please, Oliver.

Teddy Sorry, Oliver, I'm not picking you up.

Oliver (*realizing: in a bellow*) OLIVER TREEFE, SIR.

Teddy Oliver Treefsir, well come in Oliver Treefsir, what can we do for you?

Oliver They said—(*in a bellow*)—at Sprinkley's Garage a lady had been in to inquire about a boy, sir.

Eve (*to Teddy*) It must have been Molly. (*To Oliver*) When did she come in?

Oliver This afternoon—(*bellowing at Eve*)—they said. They said she said there was a car needed looking after. Mr Goldberg's Alvis.

Teddy What?

Eve Mr Goldberg's Alvis, Teddy.

Teddy Mr Goldberg hasn't got an Alvis. I've got it. Part of the deal for the house. He left it for me for what he called a consideration, he's probably bought himself a new car out of the consideration, eh, boy? Quite a business man, your Mr Goldberg. (*He laughs*)

Oliver laughs

Quite a business man. It doesn't go, boy. Needs a lot of tinkering. Can you tinker?

Oliver Yes, sir.

Teddy Can, eh? That's right, don't undersell yourself, what about a drink we got some of that stuff you English call beer somewhere and you look to be at the beer-guzzling age, eh, Evie? Like one? (*He goes to the drinks trolley*)

Oliver Well, no thank you very much, sir.

Teddy Good . . .

Teddy exits to the corridor

Eve Did the lady mention any special time to call, Oliver?

Oliver They said she said the evening would be best, Missus.

Eve I see. And was it only about the car?

Oliver Well, they said she said it would be a bit of driving and helping about the garden and odd-jobs. They said it was a proper job, Missus.

Eve (*taking a piece of paper and a pencil from the sideboard*) Well, I'm afraid Mrs Treadley isn't here at the moment, but I'll take down your details and let her have them. Who can give you references, Oliver? (*She sits in an armchair*)

Oliver Well, there's Sprinkley's.
Eve And anyone else?

Teddy enters with a mug and a bottle of beer, goes to the drinks trolley, and starts to open the beer. When it opens, and foams over, he interpolates "Damn" into his speech and mops up the beer with his handkerchief

Teddy First thing you've got to do is make her go, second thing is to break me into her ways. I'm not used to cars like your Mr Goldberg's Alvises, especially now my balance's gone, so you'll have to show me how to handle her, whether she needs coaxing or bullying, a car's like any machine, a man's made her so she's going to have something wrong with her. I used to do a lot of driving—ever heard of the Breton Trail, that's in Nova Scotia. (*Bringing Oliver his beer*) Here, get yourself outside of that.
Oliver Thank you, sir.
Teddy That's in Nova Scotia, where the roads go straight ten yards before they turn around and go back five. In a Manson. By God I loved that car. Always knew where to tinker when she gave me trouble. Think I could get to love a car that used to belong to your Mr Goldberg, eh, that he left to rot and rust for a consideration? Eh?
Eve I was just getting down some references, Teddy.
Teddy Oh.
Eve Now who else besides Sprinkley's, Oliver?
Oliver I done some gardening with my dad . . .
Teddy Who?
Oliver My dad sir.
Teddy (*going to pour himself a drink*) Your dad—a reference from your dad? We could all get references from our dads, boy. (*He laughs*)
Oliver No, I only meant . . .
Eve Where else have you worked, Oliver?

Molly enters the conservatory, stands watching for a moment, unseen by the others

Eve Where else have you worked, Oliver?
Oliver Well—(*he pauses*)—well I did some for Mrs Shepherd, Missus, but I stopped after a bit.
Eve Indeed, why?
Molly (*entering the room*) Of course, you're the boy, aren't you, that Sprinkley's promised to send. I'm so sorry I wasn't here when you arrived, please forgive me.
Oliver That's all right, Miss.
Molly (*to Teddy and Eve*) I popped in as I was passing the garage, when the thought struck, and then it slipped my mind, sorry darlings.
Teddy Where you been, Moll, old Evie was getting worried about you, out there in the dark.
Molly Were you, darling? (*To Eve*) There was no need, it was all quite friendly and above board. Well, what have you fixed up, between the three of you?

Eve We're just sorting out the question of references.

Teddy (*rising*) Drink, Moll?

Molly Thank you, darling, I'd love one.

Teddy (*pouring Molly a drink*) We've just been trying to make out from your Oliver Treefsir here whether he's the sort that kills us.

Molly (*smiling at Oliver*) And are you the sort to kill us, Oliver?

Oliver No, Miss.

Molly There we are, what more could we ask. You see, my husband's the sort that likes to drive very fast himself, but when he's being driven he likes it to be by the sort that drives very slow, don't you, darling? But I can't drive at all, so I like everybody to drive fast, even the people in other cars.

Teddy comes over, hands Molly a drink and sits on the sofa

Thank you, darling. Now what about the gardening, are you going to do that for us too?

Oliver Well, yes, Miss, I mean if you want . . .

Molly Because we need a gardener to garden for us as well as a driver who won't kill us. Oliver, it's all in the most terrible tangle out there, some of the spring what'sits look quite alarming. What are your fingers like, can we see them?

Oliver Miss?

Molly Can we see your fingers?

Oliver puts down his mug and shows his hands, both sides, at a nod from Molly

Mmmm—yes, they look as if they could be green, you see we met a lady on the boat coming over from Canada who talked every lunch time and dinner time about gardening, and she said—do you remember, darling?

Teddy What?

Molly The herbaceous border lady, darling, she said that for gardens green fingers were quite essential, of course, and that the best way to make flowers grow was to talk to them and sing to them and even recite poems to them, now would you be willing to talk and sing and recite poems to our flowers. Oliver? (*She looks at him seriously*)

Oliver Um, well . . . (*He gives a little laugh*)

Molly Oh well—(*smiling*)—what about pulling up weeds and mowing the lawn instead?

Oliver Oh yes, Miss. I could do that. I mean, my dad does the gardening for some of them in the village in the evenings, and I've helped him.

Molly There you are then. You meet our requirements exactly, doesn't he darling? (*She sits on the sofa*)

Teddy What?

Eve Excuse me, Moll, but I haven't quite found out how you can get hold of Mrs Shepherd.

Molly Why do I want to get hold of Mrs Shepherd?

Teddy Hey, that boy's been standing there with a mitt full of beer and

you ladies haven't let him take a sip of it. You have your drink boy.
Go on.

Oliver hesitates, then raises his glass and drinks

Eve (*to Molly*) Oliver used to work for Mrs Shepherd until she let him go.
Teddy That's the boy!
Molly Why did Mrs Shepherd let you go Oliver?
Oliver (*stopping drinking*) She—well, she just said she didn't need me any
    more, that's all.
Molly Oh. And if she had needed you any more we wouldn't be able to
    have you now, would we, so you see, Evie, Mrs Shepherd was only
    acting for the best; wasn't she, Oliver, if we *can* have you now, that is?
    But omigod, how much are we to pay you?
Oliver Well, Miss, whatever—I don't know.
Molly How much did Mrs Shepherd pay you?
Oliver Two pounds a week, Miss.
Molly Two pounds a week!
Eve That would be the normal rate.
Molly But it seems a mere trifle for chauffeuring us about and not killing
    us and keeping our weeds down and our flowers up and general handy-
    manning, you would do a little handymanning, wouldn't you Oliver?
    I really think a minimum of four pounds a week, wouldn't you, darling?
Eve Four pounds!
Teddy What?
Molly Four pounds a week for Oliver, darling, includes handymanning.
Teddy Give him four and a half.
Molly Four pounds ten, Oliver, there we are. Will you come to us for that?
Oliver Yes Miss! I mean, I'll have to talk it over with my dad . . .
Molly Of course you will. But even so, I think we've got you, haven't we?
Oliver Yes, Miss.
Molly Well then, dad willing, when can you start, tomorrow?
Eve Tomorrow's Sunday.
Molly Monday then.
Oliver Yes, Miss.
Molly All settled, darling. I had to use all my wiles but I've brought him
    to it.
Teddy Another beer, boy?
Oliver Um, no thanks. (*He puts his mug on a table*)
Molly Oh, we mustn't keep him any longer. He's got important matters to
    discuss with his dad. Haven't you?
Oliver Yes, Miss.
Eve I'll see you out, Oliver. (*She leads him to the conservatory*)

Oliver is confused but Eve puts him right

Molly See you Monday, Oliver.
Teddy 'Bye there, boy.
Oliver (*shouting*) Sir.
Teddy I like the look of him.

Oliver and Eve exit

Molly Did you reallly, darling? (*She takes cigarettes and lighter from her coat pocket and lights one*) Can't say I did, pale, spotty and slightly furtive, I thought. But just the sort to know all about engines and lawn-mowers and things—(*taking off her coat*)—and one never does know how to turn people down . . . (*She drops her coat in a chair*)

Teddy Where did you go?

Molly (*putting the cigarettes and lighter on a table*) Further than I meant.

Teddy Why didn't you take me with you?

Molly (*going over to him and rumpling his hair*) You were snoozing, my sweet, I hadn't the heart to wake you—(*she kisses the top of his head, goes over to the drinks trolley with his glass, pours them both a drink*)—and it really wasn't very nice anyway, you'd have found me a terrible bore. I kept thinking I heard a tune I could write down and make into one of my silly songs, it was as if I were following it, through one field, then another, right to the river where the bridge is, I was sure it was there somewhere, like a person I was going to meet, but nobody came, (*She brings him his drink back*) nobody at all.

Teddy What? I missed all that.

Molly I was just chattering.

Eve enters, from the conservatory

Well darling, you got it all out of him, I take it. (*She pours herself a drink*)

Eve What?

Molly Mrs What'sits address and the rest of it.

Eve Mrs Shepherd's. Yes, I did. I hope you don't mind. I think she might be that lady we saw in the post office the other day, having a parcel weighed.

Molly With a ridiculous hat and false teeth?

Eve I didn't really notice her teeth.

Molly What about her ankles, did you notice those?

Eve Notice what?

Molly Weren't they very thick?

Eve I'm afraid I didn't notice her ankles, either.

Molly Then it can't have been Mrs What'sit, darling, in the post office.

Eve You've met her then?

Molly Who?

Eve Mrs Shepherd.

Teddy Who are you two nattering about?

Molly Mrs Shepherd, darling.

Teddy Who's she?

Molly (*moving to an armchair and sitting*) We haven't the slightest idea, but Eve's got her address and she's determined to find out, aren't you, darling?

Eve I'm sorry, Molly, I know it wasn't my place to interfere . . .

Molly Oh Eve!

Eve It's just that I don't think you should take people on without knowing anything about them, except what they tell you themselves.
Molly Really, darling? I don't agree, we took you on without knowing anything about you except what you told us yourself, and that's worked out quite well.
Eve I gave you three references!
Molly Yes darling, but you don't think I read them.
Eve Why ever didn't you?
Molly They were far too long, and bound to be flattering, which wouldn't have been fun, so I hired you in lieu.

Eve picks up Molly's coat and scarf and takes them out to the hall

Omigod!
Teddy What?
Molly I've offended Eve again.
Teddy What?
Molly She really is the most humourless—

Eve enters, from the hall

Teddy (*not seeing her*) When she's going to feed us, that's what I want to know.
Eve I'm on my way to the kitchen now.
Molly (*rising*) Oh darling—I was only teasing, of course I read your references, they were divine, one from the two old ladies in Richmond, one from the doctor in Kingston and one from—from—wherever, but I remember it quite well, said you were scrupulous in violet ink and couldn't manage without you and no more could we, and you were right to insist on Mrs What'sit's address, and I did rush us into the youth quite fecklessly, it was just that I felt funny about having forgotten him entirely, but I know he won't get away with anything, darling, with you to keep an eye on him, and if you ever bump into Mrs Shepherd again you can quiz her to your heart's content, all right, darling, all forgiven? Please. Pretty please with sugar on it?
Eve (*smiling*) Oh Moll. Now you're teasing me again.
Molly No I'm not, darling. I mean it. (*She takes a cigarette from the table*) Every word almost.
Eve (*still smiling*) It'll just be a few minutes, Teddy.
Teddy No rush, Evie, have another drink!
Eve Then you'll never eat.

Eve exits to the corridor

Molly (*wearily*) Omigod! (*Lights her cigarette*)

Teddy watches her. There is a pause

Teddy Hey you, come here! (*Pause*) Come on, come here, I said.

Concealing her irritation, clearly knowing what is going to happen, Molly goes over to Teddy

Molly Sir?

Teddy Now my girl, how many's that since lunch?

Molly Only one, sir.

Teddy Come on, Moll, the truth now. All the time you were gadding about out there.

Molly Well, three. (*Pause*) Four. (*Pause. She holds up five fingers*) Ten. Twenty.

Teddy (*not hearing*) Five, eh? Well, add on another four and one on top of that, makes—

He motions to Molly. She lays herself over his knees. He spanks her while counting, laughing

one—two—three—four—five—six—seven—eight—nine. Now get us another drink, girl.

Molly takes his glass with a curtsy

Molly My lord. (*She pours himself another drink*)

Teddy And another thing, girl, what about getting to the piano, all your talk about your songs and you haven't touched a key since we moved in, that was another of Mr Goldberg's considerations—he can hire himself a whole band out of that one—I was telling Eve all about your seal song and Bob Hoskins transmitting it over RCVX—(*he takes her hand as she brings him the drink*)—play it now, eh, Moll.

Molly But darling, she's getting the dinner on the table.

Teddy What? Don't want to?

Molly Not very much, darling. For one thing the piano's out of tune. And so am I. (*She looks at him from above, sadly, and touches him on the shoulders*)

She indicates that he move to the most suitable end of the sofa. He does so. She goes to the piano and starts to play "Jerusalem" uncertainly. The piano is out of tune. She makes a face, and begins to sing, very loudly but nicely—"And did those feet"

Eve enters from the corridor and stands listening

Teddy, evidently straining to hear, beats his foot out of time to the music

Teddy (*as Molly is still fading out*) There. There, Evie. She wrote it herself. What do you think of it?

Eve I think it's lovely.

Molly (*rising*) Why Evie, you're tone deaf!

Eve Perhaps I am. But I know a nice voice when I hear one. Dinner's ready.

Molly moves to Teddy, touches him on the shoulder and extends her hand. He rises and takes it

Molly leads Teddy out to the corridor. Eve follows and closes the door, as the Lights fade to a BLACKOUT.

SCENE 2

The same. A week or so later. Mid-afternoon

The room is full of sunlight, the conservatory door is open

Oliver enters through the conservatory furtively. He is wearing an open-necked shirt, baggy gardening trousers. He looks towards the kitchen, back, then towards the hall door, then goes to the sofa, on which is Molly's handbag. He opens the handbag, takes out a package of cigarettes and the lighter. He quickly extracts a cigarette, puts it in his pocket, then another, which he lights. He puts the lighter back in the handbag, closes it. He stands smoking, looking around

Eve enters from the corridor and stands watching Oliver. Oliver, suddenly conscious of another presence, turns. They stare at each other

Oliver I've finished digging up them weeds around the garage, Missus.

Eve And have you done the hedge?

Oliver No, Missus. I—I don't know where the shears is.

Eve We don't keep them in the sitting-room, Oliver. Perhaps they're under the potato sacking on the second shelf in the conservatory where I told you to put them the last time you used them, have you looked?

Oliver No, Missus.

Eve Have you put the weeds in the compost?

Oliver No, Miss

Eve Then do that first, Then the hedge. And oh, Oliver . . . (*Eve gets an ashtray, comes towards Oliver, holds it out*) In here, please.

Oliver stubs out the cigarette

Now here are two things for you to understand, Oliver. Firstly, we don't like you wandering into the house whenever you feel like it, and secondly we don't like you smoking in the house; you left a saucer full of stubs in my kitchen after your lunch today. All right?

Oliver (*sulkily*) Yes, Missus.

Eve And by the way, I'm not Missus, I'm Miss. Miss Mace. (*She attempts a more friendly tone. Little pause*) Is anything the matter?

Oliver Well, Missus—Miss. The only thing—well, I mean, I was told it was going to be fixing the Alvis and driving it mainly, that was my work, and there was a bit of gardening on the side, but I mean I've got the Alvis fixed, but I've only got to drive it twice in two weeks, it's been gardening all the time, and even painting the inside of the garage.

Eve I see. Well, Oliver, if you're not satisfied with the conditions of your employment, you're quite at liberty to leave. Is that what you want to do?

Oliver No, Missus.

Eve Miss.

Oliver No, Miss.

Eve I'm sure you don't. So you'd better get on with it, hadn't you?

Oliver (*after a pause*) Yes, Miss. (*He turns to go*)

Eve (*looking into the ashtray*) Oliver. What cigarettes do you smoke?

Oliver Any sort, Missus. Miss.

Eve Including the sort that Mrs Treadley smokes?

Oliver (*shrugging*) I don't know what sort she smokes.

Eve She smokes this sort. (*Holding up the stub*) Did you take one of hers?

Oliver No, Miss!

Eve I think you did, Oliver. That's what you were doing in here, wasn't it.

Oliver No, Miss, I never!

Eve Please don't lie, Oliver.

Molly enters from the corridor

Oliver (*as Molly enters*) I'm not lying, Miss!

Molly (*looking from one to the other*) What's going on, it sounds thrilling!

Eve I'm just trying to find out whether Oliver's been helping himself to your cigarettes.

Oliver I didn't, Miss.

Molly Oh, I do hope you didn't, Oliver, I'm terribly low and I do hate to be caught without one. Shall I check and see how I'm off? (*She goes over to handbag, opens it, looks into the cigarette package*) About a dozen, I suppose that'll do, could you remember some, Evie, if you're going shopping. (*A little pause*) Are you doing something in the garden, Oliver?

Eve empties the ashtray into the wastepaper basket

Oliver I've got to put weeds in the compost and then clip the hedge, Miss.

Molly Such a nice day for being outside.

Oliver Yes, Miss.

Oliver smirks at Eve and exits to the conservatory

Eve Molly, I know he helped himself.

Molly (*lighting a cigarette*) Yes, darling, I expect you're right.

Eve Well, if there's one thing I hate it's a pilferer. And a liar.

Molly Well, we all have our pet aversions, I detest ghastly scenes and boys getting shrill all over something extremely trivial, darling.

Eve I see.

Eve exits to the corridor

Molly (*imitating first Eve, then herself*) I see. I see. Pretty please with sugar on it. Oh God . . . Evie!

Teddy enters from the hall

Teddy Hey, Moll, you nearly let me fall asleep again, you ready?

Molly What? What for, darling?

Teddy Our walk.

Molly What walk?

Teddy Aren't you coming for a walk?

Molly But, darling, we worked it all out at lunch, now we've got the piano tuned at last I was going to try and settle to some song writing, and you were going to go for a walk.

Teddy We're going to Gwyllup, it's five miles.
Molly No, darling, we were going to *drive* to Gwyllup another day . . .
Teddy No, no, walk.
Molly Anyway, not this afternoon . . .
Teddy You're smoking again.
Molly So I am, I am.
Teddy If you don't want to, you'd better not.
Molly But I do, I do.
Teddy Then we'd better get started.
Molly No, I mean smoke. (*She stubs the cigarette out irritably*)
Teddy Do you or don't you, I can't make it out.

Eve enters from the corridor

Eve (*in the doorway*) I'm just going to do the shopping.
Teddy What?
Eve I've got down tomatoes, oranges, cauliflower, the beef to be collected, four skewers . . .
Molly Oh, darling, do come in properly, it can't be any good for your throat—baying at me from over there.
Teddy I'm going to walk to Gwyllup. The question is whether you are.
Eve (*frostily*) I'm sorry. I didn't mean to bay at you.
Teddy I can perfectly well go by myself.
Eve I just wanted to know if you wanted to add anything.
Molly Add anything? To the skewers and the four cauliflowers?
Eve To the shopping list.
Teddy When you two have sorted it out, whatever it is that's so important to you, I'll be upstairs in my room. I don't want to keep interrupting you ladies when you're nattering about something important.

Teddy exits to the hall, slamming the door

Molly Omigod! We go to all the trouble of getting that little man over from Guilford so that I can play the piano properly at last, and perhaps even who knows? compose a song, and when I actually at last arrange to spend an afternoon at the piano, I find myself harassed with tales about youths stealing cigarettes, and grown men demanding to be taken for walks—it's too much, it's too, too much! (*She takes out a cigarette, lights it*)

Eve turns away, her face working. Molly looks at her, looks away angrily, draws on her cigarette

Sorry darling. Didn't mean to be ratty. Forgive please. (*A little pause*) Pretty please, with sugar on it.
Eve I expect it *is* all my fault. *I'm* sorry, Molly. The truth is, I've got a bit of a headache, this weather's a little too close for me. (*She attempts a little laugh*) That always means it's going to rain. Sorry, Moll.
Molly Oh poor darling, can I get you an aspirin?
Eve No—nothing does any good until it rains.
Molly Anyway, you mustn't think of going to the shops—why don't you have a nice lie down?

Eve Oh, I'll be all right. Really. I shouldn't have made such a fuss over
Oliver.

Molly Someone's got to make fusses for us, darling, and as you're the
only grown-up in the house, it'd better be you. We are childish, aren't
we, Teddy and I?

Eve Of course you're not.

Molly Yes we are.

Eve Well—I've always liked children.

Molly Really, darling? I wouldn't have thought you'd much to do with
them before.

Eve Oh yes. I helped to look after some once. A long time ago.

Molly Did you? (*Abruptly*) I'd like a child. Do you think it's too late for
me?

A little pause. Eve looks embarrassed

I mean adopt one of course. Now that I'm back in England—home
again. One could easily adopt one, couldn't one? What do you think?

Eve I think it's the most marvellous idea!

Molly After all, if we keep this place on, we've lots of room. He could
have the small room as a bedroom, and the room opposite as a play-
room and I could move across the hall to be next to him—and even
if we don't stay here we could find somewhere else just as big—you
see how I've been working it out?

Eve Oh Moll!

Molly And you wouldn't run away if we did?

Eve I'd love it! And what does Teddy think?

Molly Oh, I haven't mentioned it to him yet. One thing at a time for
the poor darling—first England, then a child, then if we get on with that
one perhaps another to go with it and so on and on, we may end up
with a flock of them—(*laughing*)—we'd have to keep some out in the
fields!

Eve (*laughing*) Oh Moll!

Teddy enters from the hall carrying his stick

Teddy I'm not going to doze through the afternoon; have you two fixed
it all between yourselves, yet?

Molly Oh, yes, darling, completely. Haven't we, Evie?

Eve (*smiling*) Yes.

Teddy Then you're ready to hike to Gwyllup? Or do I go on my own?

Molly Oh, darling, do you mind if I try out the lovely piano you've had
fixed for me? Do you?

Teddy You're saying no?

Molly Darling, I will, if you like.

Teddy I'm going anyway, as that's what we arranged.

Molly Besides, Evie says it's going to rain, and you know how bad that
can be for your ears—why don't you take a little local stroll.

Teddy I'm going to Gwyllup. (*Pause*) I'm going to Gwyllup.

Molly (*hesitating*) Then at least take your raincoat and your mackintosh hat.
Teddy What?
Molly Your raincoat and mackintosh hat.
Teddy What for? It's not going to rain.

Teddy stamps out through the conservatory

Molly Oh damn, damn, what shall I do, if it rains into his ears—and he *will* go to Gwyllup too, he's so stubborn—and if I go after him now he'll just stump angrily along . . .
Eve I'll take them to him. (*She runs to the hall left, returns at once with Teddy's hat and coat*)
Molly Oh thank you, darling. But really somebody ought to go with him, I know it's a lot to ask—will you?

Eve hesitates, then smiles

Eve Of course, Moll.
Molly You are a darling—and they say Gwyllup's very beautiful.
Eve (*running through the conservatory, with hat and coat, calling*) Oliver— Oliver—run after Mr Treadley, tell him to wait a minute, hurry, hurry!

Eve exits

Molly stands listening for a moment, then goes into the conservatory, stands watching, still visible to the audience, then returns. She goes to the cigarettes, picks one out, lights it, puffs on it. She sits down to smoke. After a moment gets up, stands uncertainly, kicks off her shoes, then wanders over to the radio, turns it on, bangs the top to bring the music on, moves to the sofa table and glances at some magazines, goes and switches the radio off, moves to the drinks trolley, stubs out her cigarette, pours herself a gin, drinks, pours another, goes to the sofa and sits

Molly Alone at last. (*Pause, then in a desolate voice*) Omigod! (*Pause*) Omigod!

Oliver appears in the conservatory. He is carrying the coat and the mackintosh hat.

Molly doesn't notice him. Oliver clears his throat

(*looking at him*) Oh hello. He sent them back, did he?
Oliver Yes, Miss. He said to say he doesn't need them. And he says thank you, um, for . . .
Molly What?
Oliver Well, Evie, Miss.
Molly (*smiling wryly*) Thank you. Well, sling them—sling them over there somewhere, would you?

Oliver puts them on an armchair

And how's everything in the garden?

Oliver I got the weeds on the compost. I'm going to start on the hedge.
Molly How lucky—to have something you've got to do.
Oliver Yes, Miss.

*Slight pause. Oliver goes into the conservatory, clatters about, just in sight.
Molly looks towards the conservatory, watches*

Oliver Just getting the shears, Miss. (*He holds them up*)
Molly (*with authority*) Come in for a moment, Oliver, please.

Oliver comes back into the room, carrying the shears

Two, Oliver.
Oliver Miss?
Molly (*holding up two fingers*) You took two of my cigarettes, Oliver.
Oliver I didn't! Miss, I swear . . .
Molly Oh Oliver, don't please. It makes you sound like a goose when you
  protest—you honk.
Oliver But . . . (*He stops*)
Molly (*getting cigarettes, holding the package out to Oliver*) Here, have
  another one.
Oliver No thank you, Miss.
Molly Oh go on. You mustn't mind my knowing about your being a liar,
  I lie all the time, all the time, about lots of things, about cigarettes too.
  I promise I won't smoke more than five a day, my husband thinks it's
  bad for my health, but of course I sneak extra ones, like now with you,
  he'd have a fit if he could see me puffing away. Do you know what he'd
  do? He'd put me across his knee and spank me, Oliver. Yes, he
  would. What do you think of that?
Oliver Well Miss . . . (*He gives a strange laugh*)
Molly Now I've told you all that, you've got to take one, haven't you?

Oliver hesitates, then takes a cigarette

Molly (*handing him the lighter*) I bet your dad doesn't put you across his
  knee and spank you, at least not any more, does he?
Oliver No, Miss. (*He laughs again, lights his cigarette, and returns the
  lighter*)
Molly You did take them, didn't you?
Oliver Yes, Miss.
Molly There, now we've both confessed. But I'm very sorry, Oliver, now I
  shall have to punish you. You do realize that, don't you, you can't
  pinch my cigarettes and then lie and bluster about it and not expect
  punishment, can you? (*She allows a long pause*) Sit down please, Oliver.

Oliver, after a moment, sits

Do you know what I'm going to do to you?

Oliver shakes his head

I'm going to teach you a lesson, Oliver. I'm going to make you sit here
and talk to me. (*She laughs*) Just for a little, do you mind?

Oliver (*smiling*) No Miss. Except there's the hedge and she goes on at me.
Molly Oh, *her*! Don't worry about her, Oliver, I'll protect you from her!
 (*Pause*) Tell me, do you think it's going to rain?
Oliver Yes, Miss.
Molly Oh don't say that. Why?
Oliver Because it feels like rain. And my dad said it would.
Molly And is your dad always right?
Oliver Usually, Miss.
Molly About everything, or just about the weather?
Oliver Well, about the weather, anyway, Miss.
Molly How does he know, by sniffing the air, or holding his finger up or
 rising at six for shepherd's warning?
Oliver No, Miss.
Molly How then?
Oliver He listens to the radio, Miss, at breakfast.

There is a pause

Molly Well, clever old dad. (*Laughing*) I bet you don't dare lie to him.
Oliver Oh no, Miss.
Molly What about?
Oliver Miss?
Molly What do you lie to him about?
Oliver I said I didn't, Miss.
Molly Yes, that was a lie to me. What do you lie to him about? Come on,
 Oliver, do tell me. Please, pretty please. Because I know you do.
Oliver How, Miss?
Molly Because if we didn't lie to people we love and live with, we wouldn't
 be able to love and live with them. See.

She rises, goes to the drinks trolley and pours herself a gin, studying Oliver

Oliver (*after a pause*) Well, only about Guilford. What I do over at
 Guilford. That's all.
Molly And what *do* you do over at Guilford?

*By almost imperceptible degrees, the stage darkens to suggest the sky
darkening*

 Oh of course, you've got a girl there. (*She drinks*)
Oliver Well . . . (*He shrugs*)
Molly Haven't you?
Oliver Not any more. There was a girl. I used to have tea with her some-
 times.
Molly Only tea?
Oliver Yes. She worked in a tea shop.
Molly (*drinking again*) And is that all you did with her?
Oliver We went to the pictures sometimes.
Molly Were you lovers?
Oliver What?
Molly Lovers.

There is a pause

  Here—(*she hands Oliver her own drink*)—have a sip of this.
Oliver What is it?
Molly A truth drink. To help you tell me whether you were lovers. It's
  all right, I swear I won't tell your dad if you promise not to tell mine.
  Husband. Sip and tell, Oliver.

Oliver sips

Oliver Well—(*sips again*)—no, Miss.
Molly No, won't tell, or no, weren't lovers?
Oliver Weren't—um, lovers.
Molly Oh dear, oh dear, why not?
Oliver (*laughing, embarrassed*) Don't know anything about any of that.
Molly Any of what? (*She goes over to him, takes the shears off his lap,
  puts them on the floor*) There. Any of what?
Oliver My dad wouldn't stand for any of that. He'd kill me if I did any-
  thing like that.
Molly (*standing close to him*) Then what happened between yourself and
  this girl, what was her name?
Oliver Rosie, Rosie Hitchens. Well—just one day she turned around
  when I went over and said her mum didn't want her to see me any more.
Molly And she didn't?..
Oliver (*after a pause*) No.
Molly (*after a pause*) Poor Oliver. Poor Rosie Hutchings, come to that.
  (*She goes to the drinks trolley, stubs out her cigarette, and pours herself
  a fresh drink, keeping the bottle*)
Oliver Hitchens. Her name was.
Molly Is your mother dead?
Oliver Yes, Miss. When I was born.
Molly You're terribly fond of your dad, aren't you? Tell me, what do you
  do together? I mean in the evenings, or the week-ends?
Oliver Well—we go shooting.
Molly Do you, oh dear, what do you shoot?
Oliver Only rabbits.
Molly *Only* rabbits? Oh Oliver. And do you kill many of them?
Oliver Quite a few. My dad's a good shot. I'm not bad.
Molly What do you think, when you see them dead?
Oliver That they're dead, Miss. Dead rabbits. For pie.
Molly Have you got a dog? (*She goes to Oliver with the gin bottle*)
Oliver We had one once, Miss.
Molly What happened to it?
Oliver It got run over.
Molly And what did you think, when you saw it dead.
Oliver It was in the middle of the Guilford road, where all the lorries run.
  My dad took me down to see it, lying there squashed, I was only six
  about.
Molly Why did he do that?
Oliver To show me what happened if I was careless on the road.

Molly Omigod, Oliver! And what did you say, when you saw it there?
Oliver I said—(*he thinks*)—were we going to have it for lunch.
Molly You didn't!
Oliver No, Miss. We had it for supper.
Molly (*after a moment laughing*) You're making fun of me! That's nice. *She pours more gin into Oliver's glass*) There! You see how it helps. And me. (*She pours some into her own*) Because now I'm going to tell you why I hate to think of shooting rabbits even, and you mustn't laugh at me, promise? (*She puts the bottle on the table by the sofa, and sits*)
Oliver Miss.
Molly You see, I hate anything being killed by people. Ever since I heard about something very dreadful—about how these great Canadian men with their red necks and tartan caps on their heads drive down to the beach in their trucks and they catch the seals, the mother seals and the baby seals, and they beat their heads in with clubs and hammers. Yes they do, Oliver, and sometimes the mothers stay a little way out in the sea, watching, while these—these men!— skin their babies while they're still alive often, skin them for their furs. Dreadful. Dreadful. They have such big eyes and they stare at their babies . . . D'you see, Oliver? (*She looks at him intently*) I wrote a song about it. It was broadcast on the radio over there, and played right across Nova Scotia. But it didn't stop them. That's when I knew I couldn't live in Canada any more, amongst people like that. So don't shoot any rabbits ever again. Please don't, Oliver. Pretty please. With sugar on it. (*There is a pause*) Oh I know, you've got to, for your dad's sake. You'll just have to try to miss them, that's all. For my sake. Aim—(*She raises her arm at Oliver, jerks at the last second*)—sideways. (*She laughs*) But don't hit your dad. For his sake. Are you happy with us?
Oliver Oh yes, Miss.
Molly I watch you sometimes, Oliver. Did you know that? When you're in the garden. As busy as bees. Mowing the lawn yesterday. I watched you from an upstairs window. And then on your knees weeding this morning. But I haven't seen you recite poetry to the flowers. No. And sometimes you even look a trifle—sulky. There. I've said it. As if you weren't truly and really deeply happy with us. Why not, Oliver?
Oliver I am, Miss. (*Pause*) Well.
Molly No, go on. On. (*She tops up his glass, then her own*)
Oliver She gets at me a lot, Miss.
Molly Oh, she gets at us all a lot, pay her no mind, we don't. When she gets at me I pay her out my very best smile and say forgive me, Evie, pretty please, with sugar on it. You can try that. Because then you can ignore her and be rude to her or whatever you want. What else is wrong?
Oliver Nothing, Miss. Well.
Molly On, Oliver. On.
Oliver Well, only about the car, that's all. I mean I was taken on to do the car, but now I've got it fixed up I've only taken it out twice, the rest of it's been gardening and painting the garage and the other day it was sash cords even, she made me do.

Molly I'm so glad you've told me this, Oliver. I'll have a word with Teddy when he gets back. (*She pours herself another drink*) I promise you more outings in the car. I never break my promises you know.

Oliver Oh, I don't really mind. It's just that that's what I thought I was being taken on to do mainly and well, they make jokes about it at Sprinkley's and up at the pub, because my dad told them all I was going to be a chauffeur and they say if you're a chauffeur where's your uniform. My dad doesn't like that.

Molly If your dad doesn't like it, that settles it. Although I don't know about a uniform—I don't know if I'd like you so much in a uniform. Will you teach me to drive, Oliver, and keep it a secret from dad. Will you?

Oliver Yes, Miss.

Molly And then when you've taught me I'll show him I can. Eh? Oliver? (*She laughs*) If you promise to teach me then you shall have a uniform—even though I like you just as you are, Oliver. I like you very much. You do know that, don't you?

They stare at each other

Do you like him?

Oliver Who?

Molly Teddy.

Oliver Yes, Miss.

Molly So do I. Even though he calls you boy and Ollie and Oliver Treefsir?

Oliver Oh, I don't mind that. It's just his way.

Molly Because he's deaf, you see. It's so sad. Because people when they're deaf can't have normal friendly conversations with each other, as we're having, so they have to find little tricks of their own to show normal friendliness, and to hide their deafness too. And he's very friendly. More than normally.

Oliver He doesn't really—

Molly What?

Oliver (*hesitatingly*) put you over his knee, does he?

Molly D'you mind?

Oliver Miss. (*He laughs*) He doesn't! Does he?

Molly (*rising*) I'm so worried, Oliver, about his getting his ears wet. And your saying it's going to rain . . . (*She goes over to the window, looks out*) It's darker, getting darker. It is raining a little. Oh damn! Oh poor Teddy. But it's delicious, too, isn't it, the two of us snug inside, talking and drinking, while outside—(*shivering*)—delicious. (*She takes a gulp of gin*) Do you like me, Oliver?

Oliver Miss?

Molly Or do you think I'm just a silly old vamp, do you?

Oliver No, Miss.

Molly What then? Say it. You must say it. I said it to you.

Oliver Like you, Miss.

Molly But I don't frighten you, do I?

Oliver No, Miss.

Molly We'll have another cigarette, shall we?

She goes with cigarettes, offers one to Oliver, lights it for him. She stares at him, takes a step around the side of the sofa, puts her foot on the shears, stumbles, cries out

Oliver (*rising*) What is it, Miss, what is it?
Molly I've cut myself—my foot . . . (*She tries to see the sole of her foot*) Can you see?

Oliver, bending some distance away, stares

Look properly—take it . . . (*She stretches out her leg*)
Oliver (*taking her foot gingerly*) I can't see any cut, Miss.
Molly But it's wet—I can feel the bleeding . . .
Oliver No, Miss—that's your drink—I can smell it—that's all . . .
Molly But it hurts, oh God, it hurts . . . (*She loses balance, hops*)
Oliver Miss—Miss . . . (*He lets go of Molly's leg*)

Molly stumbles towards Oliver, who puts out his arms to catch her

Molly Oh Oliver—(*clinging to him*)—it did hurt—it did . . .
Oliver (*in alarm*) Miss.
Molly Oliver—don't be frightened. Don't be.
Oliver Miss?

Molly begins to kiss Oliver, ravenously. Oliver clumsily responds. The Lights fade to a BLACKOUT *to the sound of rain. The rain continues through the darkness*

SCENE 3

The same. About an hour later

The lights come up to greyness. It is still raining heavily

The sofa cushions are on the floor. Teddy's raincoat is spread on the sofa seat, waterproof side up. Oliver sits, trouserless, huddled at the end of the sofa. Molly is by the piano, finishing dressing

Molly Oh that rain, that bloody rain—but they'll have found somewhere in the village—or a tree—the poor man—next time I'll check the weather with your dad or the wireless. Oliver—(*She goes over to him*)—Oliver darling, what is it? (*She sits down on the sofa next to him, tries to remove Oliver's arm from his face*) Oliver—don't—you mustn't—here, here . . . (*She pulls his arm away*) Why are you? Is it because you're unhappy? Are you unhappy?
Oliver (*shaking his head*) No, Miss.
Molly Because you're happy then?

Oliver, crying, turns his face away

(*taking his face in her hands*) Because you're happy?

Oliver Miss. I don't know, Miss.

Molly (*cuddling him*) There Oliver, nothing to cry for, nothing to cry for. I'm glad, I am, yes I am, and I want you to be happy, but you mustn't cry . . .

Oliver (*embracing her with sudden and desperate passion*) Please, Miss, please, Miss, please, Miss . . .

Molly What, darling? What?

Oliver You won't send me away, Miss?

Molly No, no—of course not—just for now—just for a little while— but there'll be other times, I promise you. Lots of other times, but we mustn't let them find out, must we? They wouldn't understand, and I wouldn't want to hurt Teddy, he loves me, you know, and I must care for him too, mustn't I, and not let him be hurt, so now I've got to put everything right and you must finish getting dressed, darling, help me by being as quick as you can, darling, before they come back—do you understand, darling? Do you?

Oliver nods

Go on, then. Go on, my darling. (*She rises, picks up a sofa cushion from the floor, and places it on the sofa*)

Oliver puts on his trousers and boots. Molly replaces the rest of the sofa cushions and picks up her shoes, then precedes Oliver to the hall door

(*During this*) Now you go on, my darling—there's a good boy . . .

Oliver follows Molly, buttoning his fly. She kisses him swiftly. Oliver exits, but returns immediately to embrace her passionately

I'll see you soon. I promise. And I never break promises. Go, Oliver.

Molly takes Oliver out to the hall

There is a door slam

Molly returns. At the same time, Teddy is heard in the conservatory, he opens the door and enters, soaking wet, followed by Eve, also wet. Eve removes her shoes before entering

Molly Omigod—darling, what happened?

Teddy Well, here I am, Moll, back from a stroll in your nice quiet country-side, right in the middle of the fields, eh Evie, then wham, right out of your nice quiet clouds, wham, wham, wham! (*He laughs*)

Molly Darling, you must get into some dry clothes.

Eve And a hot bath!

Teddy And there we were, Evie and me, licking across the field in the dark, sheets of it coming down, and there was this tree Evie saw, on a bank and a ditch running under it, anyway wouldn't pass in Nova Scotia for a river—(*he laughs*)—and I swayed on the edge, eh, Evie?

Molly Darling, tell me afterwards, get changed now?

Teddy Felt like minutes, rocking and swaying, and Evie had hold of my arm pulling me back, but a hand shot out of nowhere and down I went.

Molly A hand?

Teddy And down I went, right, Evie?

Molly You were pushed?

Teddy And down I went, right, Evie, Evie almost coming with me. (*He laughs*) So don't you two talk to me about your friendly English countryside again, we've got bob-cat, bear and skunk in Nova Scotia but we don't have anything you can't see or hear or understand come up behind you and tumble you into the mud for no damn reason—raining inside my skull. (*He removes his ear-piece and the unit from his pocket*) Damn thing, damned thing, battery soaking—get it fixed, fixed tomorrow. (*He sways slightly*) Hey, Moll!

Molly (*moving to Teddy and feeling his brow*) He's trembling—darling! He's feverish—come on, darling, we must get you to a bath and bed —come along. (*She pulls Teddy towards the door*)

Teddy I'm all right—I'm all right . .

Teddy pushes Molly aside and exits to the hall

Molly follows Teddy to the door, then turns back to Eve

Molly I told you to make him take his raincoat and his mackintosh hat! *I told you!*

Molly goes out to the hall

Eve stands for a moment, then, automatically, bends and picks up Teddy's hat

Eve (*in an emotional voice*) It's jolly well not fair!

The Lights fade to a BLACKOUT, *as—*

the CURTAIN *falls*

ACT II

The same. A week or so later. Mid-afternoon. The sun is shining

Eve is sitting on the sofa with some knitting on her lap. She is staring ahead. There is the sound of a door closing, off, up left. Then quick footsteps. Eve starts knitting. Molly, carrying a scarf, enters from the hall

Molly Hello darling, seen my handbag?

Eve On the sofa.

Molly You are clever. (*She picks up her handbag from the sofa*)

Eve You usually leave it on the sofa. Have you got Teddy's drops?

Molly Oh, yes, here they are. (*She fishes them out of handbag, puts them on the table*)

Eve He always needs them first thing, when he wakes.

Molly I know, poor darling. Isn't that growing—Teddy'll be so thrilled. I wish I could knit. (*She puts the scarf in her handbag*)

Eve Do you? It's not difficult.

Molly No, I suppose it can't be, as so many dolts can. It's one of those activities I always thought I'd find myself doing when I grew up—like putting on grey hair and wrinkles.

Eve Indeed?

Molly Oh, darling, I didn't mean . . . (*She laughs*)

Eve (*smiling coldly*) Are you going out?

Molly Yes, I've got an appointment with Oliver for a driving lesson. What about you?

Eve Oh, no. I don't think Teddy should be left alone at the moment.

Molly But darling, he's asleep, I've just checked.

Eve Yesterday when you were having a driving lesson and I was down here he woke up and thought he was alone in the house. He was quite fretful for a good half hour.

Molly I must say, darling, that doesn't sound like a good half hour to me. (*She hesitates*) In that case why don't you go out and I'll stay in, it's your turn. (*She sits in an armchair*)

Eve No, I'd as soon get on with this. Besides Oliver will be expecting you.

Molly Oh, I can always find something else for him to do.

Eve I'm glad he's settling down so well. Since you moved him into the house.

Molly Hasn't he been a godsend.

Eve Yes. Mrs Shepherd says he's funny in the head. She came around yesterday morning. She'd heard he was living in so she came around especially to warn us. She said he was funny in the head. That's why

they dismissed him. Her husband caught him in their bedroom, going through her underwear drawer.
Molly Oh, don't you worry, darling. Your underwear drawer is quite safe. Oliver's told me all about it.
Eve I see. You don't think it peculiar even then?
Molly Nothing like as peculiar as Mrs Shepherd trekking all the way up here to tell us about it.
Eve Oh well, as long as *you* don't mind ...
Molly No, I don't mind, darling. Not at all. And if you're not keen to go out I'll get some fresh air. (*She gets up and goes towards the conservatory*)

Eve watches her

Eve (*as Molly gets to the conservatory door*) Oh by the way, Molly, as soon as Teddy's better I shall be leaving. (*A little pause*) I thought I should tell you now, so you'd have time to find someone more suitable.
Molly More suitable to what, darling?
Eve To what's going on in this house.
Molly (*moving back into the room*) What *is* going on in this house?
Eve Wasn't Oliver in your room last night?
Molly Yes, he did look in to say good night and to ask how Teddy was.
Eve He stayed the whole night.

Molly makes to exclaim

Please don't lie to me, Moll. I couldn't bear it. I heard Teddy stumbling down the hall at midnight. It was only by the grace of God that I managed to stop him opening the door on the two of you. He'd had a nightmare, and wanted comforting. Thank God *he* couldn't hear what I heard.

There is the honk of a motor horn from outside

Molly Omigod! Thank you, Evie!
Eve But it wasn't you I was thinking of, it was Teddy.
Molly I know. Thank you. (*She puts down her handbag and scarf*) Teddy and I don't sleep together, surely you've realized that.
Eve But—but he's still your husband. You married him.
Molly Yes, And I do my very best to make him happy, haven't you noticed? I get drunk with him, and cuddle him, and let him slap me on the bottom —all—all that. It's enough for Teddy. It's not always enough for me. (*She takes a cigarette from her bag*)

Eve You mean—you've done this before?
Molly From time to time. Though not as often as I want to. (*She lights her cigarette*)
Eve Oh, you sound so hard—so hard.
Molly Do I, darling? Sorry. You've been a companion-housekeeper to a wicked woman, darling, you see. I need my sex. There. I've said it.
Eve Then you had no right to marry Teddy.
Molly Hadn't? He wanted me to.

Eve But what did you marry him for? His money?

Molly I admit I wouldn't have if he'd been an impoverished ... (*She gestures*)

Eve Garage hand. Like Oliver Treefe, you mean?

Molly Well, unlike Oliver, Teddy would have been a sixty-year-old impoverished garage hand when I married him, so I probably wouldn't have married him, no.

Eve I don't understand.

Molly What, darling? What don't you understand?

Eve You who could have married anybody. . .

Molly Not when I married Teddy. Don't forget he *was* only sixty, and I was *all* of thirty—and he was quite a dynamic Halifax businessman and I was one of those, you know, glamorous English divorcees that end up in countries like Canada on spec.

Eve I didn't know you'd been married before.

Molly Gets worse and worse, doesn't it, darling. Yes. Married before. Sorry. There were no children though, other than the two of us. Then he began to grow up, and left me for someone who would look after him properly. I've never been very good at getting meals on tables and organizing homes and curtains and housekeeping—all the things you're so good at doing. He's a solicitor in Harrow now, I think it is, with no doubt children and all the rest of the things—(*she gestures*)—he couldn't imagine me providing him with. (*Pause*) Actually, I did almost manage a child, but it miscarried. He blamed me for that—my fecklessness— because we'd been to a party and I drank a mite too much and slipped and fell down the stairs. He rather hated me—(*Pause*) So after I'd set him free I took a plunge, and went off to Canada, where I just managed to keep my head above water doing lady-like little jobs and being glamorous and English—all the right things to be if one wanted one of those ghastly Canadian men as a lover, you know, balding and fattening, but no good for husbands, because they were already. Until Teddy came along. I was working as a part-time receptionist sort of person who did a little piano playing and drinking in the hotel and he was the first eligible male I've infatuated. Except there is just this little thing wrong with him, I don't know what, but he doesn't have sex, I don't believe he ever has. But apart from that and already beginning to deafen he was quite dynamic and infatuated. There. Now do you understand, Evie?

Eve I suppose I might, oh I wouldn't approve but I might understand if it were some—man you'd—you'd—but Oliver Treefe! Can't you see what he is?

Molly What is he, darling? Other than peculiar in the head?

Eve Well, for one thing he's—he's twenty years younger than you.

Molly Is that worse than being almost thirty years older?

Eve But he's—he's completely uneducated. He's not even particularly nice to look at. Even I can see that. He's a common, loutish ...

Molly Stop it, Eve. Please. The truth is, Ollie and I . .

Eve Ollie and you! Ollie and you! No, I can't stop it, I jolly well think it's disgusting. Disgusting!

Molly (*in a sudden scream*) We're all disgusting!

There is a pause

Eve (*rising*) Well *I'm* not Molly Treadley. No, *I'm* not!

Oliver enters through the conservatory. He is wearing a chauffeur's uniform carrying a cap and gauntlets

Oliver Oh, excuse me, Miss, I've been honking for you outside.
Molly Honking for me?

Eve exits to the hall

Oliver She in one of her bad moods?
Molly A touch edgy, perhaps. (*A little pause*) Look darling, I'm sorry, but I'd better not come this afternoon, after all.
Oliver Why not?
Molly Why don't you give your dad that ride you've been promising him? He's scarcely seen you this last ten days.
Oliver He's working.
Molly Well darling, anything you want to do—do. (*She smiles at him*)
Oliver I want to go out with you. You promised me, Moll. To make up for all that hanging about outside Gracey's this morning.
Molly I know darling, I'm sorry, but really I can't.
Oliver It *is* because of her, isn't it?
Molly I suppose so. Because of her and him and you and me—it's all very complicated and I'm not up to explaining it, and you wouldn't like it if I did, darling, but what it comes down to is that it would make everything worse if we skipped off right now.
Oliver It's not fair. I've been sitting out there, honking and waiting and I've changed the oil even, and now you tell me you can't come out and won't tell me why, but it's because of her and him— I know it is.
Molly Oliver!

Oliver makes to say something else

No, don't say another word, Ollie. Not now. Just go. For your sake, darling.

Oliver looks at her, starts to go through the conservatory, then turns back. Molly stubs out her cigarette

Oliver It's true, what they say, isn't it? That you hooked him for his money and car and that. That's what Sprinkley said from the beginning, the first time he saw you, and my dad's said something about you and him, he thinks it's wrong, and Bob Howells making jokes in the pub, if he pays you for every go or how many times a week you have to let him do it, they were all laughing at his jokes in the pub about him and you. All of them. That's what I have to sit and listen to.
Molly (*moving to Oliver*) Who is Bob Howells, darling?
Oliver He's Sprinkley's cousin, he . . .

Molly slaps Oliver across the face. He reels back

Molly If you ever—ever—talk to me like that again, it's back to Bob
 Howells and Sprinkley's for you, my boy.
Oliver (*in a whisper*) You wouldn't.
Molly Yes, I would, my lad. You can add some jokes of your own and
 lead the laughter, but you'll never see me again, except from a great
 distance.

She turns away. He sinks into an armchair

(*Turning back to him*) Oh Oliver, why do you get like this?
Oliver But I love you, I love you.
Molly That's all right, darling. You may love me. I want you to.
Oliver But I can't stand it when I'm not with you, when you're in here
 talking to her, or go into his room to talk to him, and I don't know
 what's going on, but I think of you and him touching you and I don't
 know, what am I to do. You see, before it was like—it was like I was
 stuck somewhere underground and—and you took me out—and now I
 want to be out all the time, but when you're not there it's like being
 stuck back down again. (*A little pause*) Last night you said I was your
 husband even. But I'm not, am I? He is, isn't he? He has you most.
Molly (*going to kneel at Oliver's feet*) But you have far more of me,
 especially now. He doesn't kiss me where you kiss me, he doesn't hold
 me as you hold me—we mustn't grudge him anything, Ollie. Not
 anything. (*A little pause*) Darling.
Oliver (*looking at her*) I'm sorry for what I said. I didn't mean it.
Molly I know. (*She rises and pulls him to his feet*) Oh my Ollie.
Oliver You still love me then, don't you?
Molly Of course I do.
Oliver You won't ever send me away, will you?
Molly When Rosie Hitchins from Guilford comes to claim you back.
Oliver Never!
Molly Well, not if I can help it.
Oliver Then I've got you, then, haven't I? (*Jubiliantly*) Got you!

*They embrace. Molly kisses him tenderly, as if he were a child. She wipes
his cheeks with her fingers, then kisses him again. The kiss becomes
passionate*

Please Moll. Come out.
Molly (*she laughs*) You're quite impossible Oliver Treefe.
Oliver You will, won't you?
Molly (*hesitatingly*) Oh why not—yes—let's . . .

*Oliver gets his hat from the chair and starts for the conservatory. Molly
collects her handbag and scarf. Eve knocks at the hall door. Molly and
Oliver stop. On the second knock, Oliver tries to pull Molly to the conservatory—she stops him*

Molly Come in.

(*Eve enters from the hall*)

Eve Excuse me. I wasn't sure whether you'd gone.

Molly Oh, that's all right, darling. We're just off.
Eve I wondered if I could have a few words with you.
Molly Of course. Oliver, wait in the car, would you. I won't be a minute.

Oliver glances suspiciously at Eve, then exits to the conservatory

Eve I think it would be better if I left as soon as possible. So I'd be grateful
  if you got back by five. I'd like to catch the six o'clock train.
Molly Would you like Oliver to drive you to the station?
Eve No thank you. I'll call for a taxi, if I may.
Molly Where are you going?
Eve To Gosport.
Molly I didn't know you had anyone in Gosport.
Eve A niece.
Molly And does she have children?
Eve Yes.
Molly You'll be able to help her with them, I suppose.
Eve They're quite grown up.
Molly Those are the ones that really need your help. (*She smiles*)
Eve If Teddy wakes I shan't say anything, I'd rather you explained.
Molly He'll miss you dreadfully. So will I, of course.
Eve I'll pack now. (*She goes towards the hall door*)
Molly (*Molly hesitates a moment*) Evie.

Eve stops, turns

Evie, please don't go! (*She runs across to her, embraces her*) I need you
  so. I do.

Eve stands stiffly for a moment, then turns and embraces Molly

Eve Oh Moll!
Molly You won't leave me, Evie. Will you?
Eve (*after a moment*) No, Moll. Not if you really need me.
Molly Oh thank you, darling. Thank you. Thank you.

*There is a sudden thumping from above, and, a moment later, the sound of
the car horn*

Teddy (*off, above*) Hey! Molly, Eve—hey!

Molly looks at Eve, appealingly

Eve You'd better go. But I can't tell lies for you, Molly Treadley. I can't
  do that.
Molly (*picking up her bag*) No, darling. I know.

Molly goes out through the conservatory

*Eve watches her go through the conservatory, stands for a moment. She
puts her hand to her forehead*

*Teddy enters from the hall. He is wearing dressing-gown and slippers, but
is without a hearing-aid*

M—C

Eve Teddy—you shouldn't be up.
Teddy Where's Moll?
Eve (*slowly and loudly*) She's gone out.

There is the sound of the car screeching down the drive

Teddy She went out this morning—where's she gone to, this time?
Eve (*hesitating*) Oh, just for a drive. (*She hides the drops in her pocket*)
Teddy What?
Eve To get your drops.
Teddy What?
Eve To get your drops. Teddy, you mustn't stay down here. (*She goes to him*)
Teddy What? (*Irritably, pulling his arm away*) Did she forget them this morning, then ?
Eve They had to make up a fresh batch—it's too cold for you down here, Teddy.
Teddy Not going back to bed with a stuffed nose—like being in a damned prison. (*He goes over, pours himself a Scotch, slops the drink, pays no attention, takes a gulp*) Can't taste the taste, only the heat. (*He sits down*) Go in the car?
Eve Yes. (*She sits and takes up her knitting*)
Teddy (*after a pause*) Saw them coming around the side of the house the other afternoon. Looked out of my window and there they were, around my side of the house, right beneath me. Like a pair of ghosts. (*He attempts to sniff*) Don't worry, not delirious, Evie. Like ghosts because I couldn't hear them. Couldn't have smelt them either, come to that. Lost my hearing, now I lost my smelling, what goes next, eh? (*He laughs*) She was laughing. He had his mouth open. Maybe shouting a joke or something. Anyway, his mouth was open.
Eve I think he has adenoids.
Teddy Great sense of humour?
Eve No, adenoids.
Teddy Knocked on my window, but they didn't hear. Went right on round. A moment later they were back again, on the other side, gravel showering every which way. Too damned fast. (*Pause*) Too damned fast. God knows what he gets up to when I can't see him. (*Pause, he sniffs*) Why didn't you tell her yesterday I was running out, you could see I was, couldn't you?
Eve I'm sorry.
Teddy What you knitting there, a coloured ladder?
Eve A scarf.
Teddy What?
Eve (*explosively*) A *scarf*! It's going to be a scarf.
Teddy Like having him around the house all the time?
Eve Who?
Teddy What's he like?
Eve Oh, I expect he's a normal boy.
Teddy What?

Eve A normal boy.
Teddy (*after a pause*) Hey, Evie—(*pause*) last night—(*he sniffs*)—you tuck
  me up in bed? Or was it a dream?
Eve I made your bed comfortable for you. The covers had slipped.
Teddy Oh. (*A little pause. Vaguely*) What? (*He attempts to blow his nose*)
  Damn! Damn! (*He sits sunken in misery*)

Eve looks at Teddy, goes on knitting, looks at him again

Eve (*suddenly*) Get rid of him, Teddy!

Teddy looks at her

Teddy (*after a pause*) What?

Eve gets up, goes over to him, takes out the bottle of drops, hands it to Teddy

Eve I can't bear to see you suffering like this.
Teddy That's all right, Evie, anyone can make a mistake. (*He takes the
  bottle, administers the drops, two to each nostril*)

Eve goes back, sits down

  Tell me something, Evie—that scarf. Is it for me?
Evie Yes.
Teddy Thank you, Evie.

There is a pause. Teddy sits staring ahead, Eve goes on with her knitting

  (*Dimly*) What?

The lights fade to a BLACKOUT.

SCENE 2

The same. A couple of hours later

*Eve is knitting, Teddy asleep on the sofa. He rouses himself, gets up heavily
and goes to the drinks trolley to pour himself a large Scotch. Molly and
Oliver enter playfully from the conservatory: they stop when they see Teddy*

Molly (*crossing to Teddy*) Darling, should you be up? Gracey said a few
  more days in bed ...
Teddy Got tired of being stuck up there in bed—thought I'd come down,
  I'm fine—hello there, boy, how are you?
Oliver Sir.
Teddy What?
Oliver All right, thank you, sir.
Teddy What about a drink? Moll? (*He dashes some gin into a glass and
  hands it her*)
Molly But, darling ...
Teddy Where you been?
Molly Oh, just for a little drive ..

Teddy What?

Molly For a little drive.

Teddy Get my drops?

Molly No, I got you a fresh bottle this morning . . .

Teddy Don't need them anyway, Evie had a bottle all the time—nice time?

Molly Except for a horrid little scene on the way back.

Teddy What?

Molly A horrid little scene.

Teddy You and him?

Molly No, darling, two louts shooting in the field past the bridge. I made Oliver stop the car and when we went over there was a rabbit, they'd only wounded it and tied its legs, can you believe? And a beastly little dog . . .

Oliver A terrier.

Teddy What?

Oliver A terrier, sir.

Teddy No good, boy, yours is the voice I'll never catch.

Molly Anyway, they just stood there while Oliver had to kill it with a stick.

Teddy Killed the dog with a stick.

Molly No, a rabbit, darling . . .

Teddy Rabbit, eh? Bet she didn't like that, eh boy?

Oliver No, sir.

Teddy Doesn't like animals being hurt, do you, Moll? Ever told you about the seals at Nanaimo, she wrote a song about it, got done across Nova Scotia because Bob Hoskins was a friend of mine, I asked him to do it for her. A good friend. (*He laughs*) Eh Moll? But she'd never even been to Nanaimo, eh Moll, but somebody told her about the seals and she made up a song out of her head, and that's how it got heard right across Nova Scotia. Nanaimo's in British Columbia, four thousand miles away. What do you think of that, eh Ollie—these ladies, seals, rabbits, songs—all the same to them, hey, boy? Out in Nova Scotia we only shoot rabbits when we can't find out Catholics. We like to shoot Catholics. (*He laughs*) Ever told you about that, Moll? When some damned fool out hunting saw the bushes move, fired into them, wounded another damned fool out hunting. Nova Scotia paper headlined the story, "Father of Nine Shot. Mistaken for rabbit." Hey. Nine kids.

Molly puts her bag on the trolley, takes out a cigarette and lights it

That's how we knew he was a *Catholic*. (*He laughs*) Wish we'd had you around, boy, to beat him to death with a stick. (*He sits on the sofa*) Hey, girl, come over here. Come on.

Molly makes an unbelieving gesture

Come on, girl. Here, I say.

Molly goes to Teddy

How many's it been, eh? How many seen her smoke, boy? Two hundred three hundred since I was laid up—say five. Let you off with five, Molly, eh?

Molly lies over Teddy's knees. He smacks her five times

One—two—three—four—five. (*He helps her off his knees*) There, letting you off lightly, eh, girl?

Oliver's face is set

Molly (*seeing Oliver's face*) Evie, is there some tea for Oliver.
Eve Come with me, Oliver.

Eve exits to the corridor

Teddy Hey, boy, something I've been meaning to ask you—that hedge you started, remember seeing you at it on my way to the ditch I fell into—how's it going, got it level?
Oliver Well, I've been doing a lot of driving. Haven't had a chance to get back to it yet.
Teddy Don't know what you're saying, boy, but I can see from your face it's an excuse, where's Mr Goldberg's Alvis, put it away?
Oliver Sir.
Teddy Where?
Oliver In the garage, sir.
Teddy (*holding out his hand*) Give me the keys, boy.
Molly Darling, I did say Oliver could give his dad a run later this evening...
Teddy The keys.

Oliver takes the keys out of his pocket, glaring at Teddy, and drops them in Teddy's hand

That's the boy. Now why don't you go to trim the hedge until the sun sets—eh? (*He gives him a friendly cuff on the shoulder*)
Molly But he hasn't had his tea . . .
Teddy What? (*He turns around, gives her a malevolent stare*)
Molly He hasn't . . . (*She breaks off*)
Teddy Well? (*He looks at Oliver*)

Oliver turns, blunders into the conservatory and picks up the shears

Teddy Hey, just a minute—

Oliver turns back to the room

There's another thing, don't need you around the house at night any more, you can go back to your daddy now, best if you move out this evening, eh?

Oliver stands staring at Teddy, then turns and goes off

Tell you the truth, Moll, don't like him. Foxy little face. Have you noticed his foxy little face?
Molly No. (*She sits on the sofa*)

Teddy Just what you said when we took him on—furtive, pasty, crooked. . .

Eve enters and moves towards the conservatory

Eve Oliver's tea is ready.
Teddy Oh, hey Eve, that boy, he's not going to be around at night—just told him to go home to his daddy.
Eve Oh.
Teddy (*going to the drinks trolley and pouring a sherry*) Come and have one of your dry-as-dust sherries, Evie. Things are getting back to rights here, going to get Moll to play us one of her tunes in a minute . . .
Eve That'll be nice. (*She sits in an armchair*)

Molly moves to Eve and speaks in a low voice

Molly Would you please leave us.
Teddy What?

Eve rises and moves to the door to the corridor

Hey, Evie, where are you going?

Eve exits

What's the matter with her? (*Pause*) Hey, Moll? Hey?

They stare at each other

Molly Why did you do that?
Teddy What?
Molly I've never known you humiliate a child before.
Teddy What?
Molly (*loudly fiercely*) I've never known you humiliate a child before.
Teddy Oh. (*Pause*) Never had one to humiliate before. (*He laughs, then goes and sits on the sofa*)

Molly watches him, then runs to him and kneels at his feet

Molly Oh Teddy—what is it? What is it?

He looks at her, turns his head away and mutters something

Molly (*taking his hand*) You're still not well, you shouldn't be up, darling —please come to bed . . .
Teddy (*grabbing her arm*) What? What? What? (*Pause*) Faces are different when they shout at the deaf. Ever thought of that, what I have to see in your faces—swelling, with effort and—and contempt. And a little trickle of noise comes out I have to make sense of. Most often I get it wrong. I can see that in your faces too. Bellowing, contempt and boredom. That's all I see on your faces, all there is to see, isn't anything else, I see what's there. Everything. All I have of my own is—is the smell of fish. Fish. Know what's ahead of me—think I don't. I've seen old men. Hate this country of yours. Small and damp like a prison. Shambling about— cocktail cabinet to armchair, armchair to cocktail cabinet, pyjamas bagging out around the arse, crutch stained with pee-dribble, cocktail

cabinet to lavatory to armchair, to—to—Eve tucking me in, like I was a kid—teeth out in a glass—and all the time your faces swelling and bellowing, boredom and contempt, hate it, hate it, hate you all— what you've done to me—why didn't you leave me alone, never needed you, don't need you, natter, natter, natter. (*He drops her arm and sits staring ahead*) Brought me here to die. Know you. Know what you are. (*He sits staring ahead, shrunken and malevolent*)

Molly Omigod!

Teddy What? (*He sees Oliver in the conservatory and laughs*) Ha! Look, there he is—back—look at him—little . . . (*He rises, and moves to the conservatory*) Get up . . .

Oliver moves in from the conservatory towards Teddy, holding the shears. Molly remains kneeling by the sofa

Hah! You're fired, boy! Fired! Mine. Belongs to me. Mr Goldberg's Alvis, too—do what I like with her—everything, you're fired, fired. (*He spits into Oliver's face, then returns, laughing, and sits in the armchair*) Hey, Moll . . .

Oliver, with a strangled scream, rushes at Teddy and stabs him three times with the shears, then drops them. At the sounds Molly, still kneeling, turns her head and watches in horror. Oliver sees the blood on his hands and realizes what he has done

Oliver Didn't mean it, didn't mean it, Miss—he made me—

Molly rises and crosses slowly to Teddy

—made me—what'll I do . . . (*Pause*) Miss!

Oliver drops the shears and runs through the conservatory

Molly Poor Teddy. (*She puts her arms round Teddy*) Poor old man. (*She sees the blood on her hands*) Eve! Eee-eeve! Eee-ve!

Eve enters from the corridor

Eee-eeve! He's alive, he's still alive. Get help, you fool. Get help!

BLACKOUT

SCENE 3

The same about an hour later

Teddy's body and the armchair have been removed. Greaves and a Police Constable are standing talking by the piano. Eve enters from the hall. Greaves nods to the Constable, who takes up a position by the conservatory

Eve It's just as I said. She's asleep. Dr Gracey gave her a very strong sedative. There's not the slightest chance that you'll be able to see her until the morning.

Greaves Then perhaps you'll answer a few questions, Miss Mace.

Eve I'm afraid I can't. I must get back to Mrs Treadley.

Greaves But if she's asleep?

Eve Dr Gracey asked me to sit by her. She was in a state of shock. And if she wakes . . .

Greaves Miss Mace, I don't quite understand your position in the household.

Eve I'm—the companion-housekeeper.

Greaves I see. And are you the only staff?

Eve Well, there's a boy from the village, to help with the gardening and drive the car from time to time.

Greaves And was he here when the accident happened?

Eve No. He'd gone home.

Greaves So there was just you, and Mr and Mrs Treadley?

Eve Yes.

Greaves And did you see the accident?

Eve No. I was in the kitchen.

Greaves So Mr and Mrs Treadley were alone in here?

Eve Yes. Now I really must . . .

Greaves Where are the shears?

Eve The shears?

Greaves Dr Gracey said the wound had been caused by gardening shears.

Eve Oh. Oh yes—they're in there. On the second shelf under the potato sacking.

Greaves Why?

Eve Because that's where they belong.

Greaves But they must have been covered in blood.

Eve Of course they were. I washed it off.

Greaves But that was important evidence.

Eve Evidence of what? It was an accident.

Molly (*off*) Eve . . .

Eve Now I really must go to Mrs Treadley—

Molly (*off*) Eve . . .

Eve —you can come back tomorrow.

Molly enters from the hall in a nightdress and dressing-gown

Molly Ee-eeve . . . Oh, who are you?

Eve (*going to her*) Molly—you shouldn't be up, you must get back to bed.

Molly Who are they?

Greaves Police, Mrs Treadley. I wonder if we could . . .

Eve They were just leaving. Now come along . . .

Molly The police. Oh I'm so glad you've come, I want to make a complaint.

Eve Molly . . .

Molly No, darling, I'm going to. About those ambulance men. They were rough—far too rough—I told them to be careful, but one of them pushed me away, yes, actually *pushed* me, didn't he, Evie, when I was trying to help them lift him—and then they said he was dead but he wasn't, not until they came and heaved him about and wouldn't let me—he was alive, wasn't he, Evie. I know because I held him you see, and I could feel something pumping under his blood, quite strongly, there was life in him and then they came—it must have been them, something they did—and they were very rude too, weren't they, Evie, do you know they refused to let me ride to the hospital with him, my own husband and they refused—so I want to report them, will you report them for me?

Greaves I shall certainly question them, Mrs Treadley.

Molly Will you? Oh thank you—thank you, you're very—would you like a drink?

Greaves No thank you, Mrs Treadley.

Molly (*to the Constable*) What about you, I'm sure you'd like one, wouldn't you?

Greaves We're not allowed to drink on duty, Mrs Treadley.

Eve Now come, my dear—back to bed . . .

Molly (*going to the drinks trolley and pouring a neat gin*) No, no, just a minute, Evie, I'd like a—I can't sleep you know—it's no good—I've tried and tried—you're sure you're not allowed—will you excuse me if I just have a little, a teeny weeny . . .

Eve You really mustn't drink—Dr Gracey gave you a sedative . . .

Molly Well, it hasn't worked, darling, has it, I mean here I am full of beans, God knows what he gave me, unless it was beans of course—(*she laughs*)—and wasn't he so incompetent, he was, he really was, not that I want to get him into trouble, he's old and easily upset, all he could do was shake those dreadful wattles of his, he had no idea, no idea at all. I can't help thinking if we'd got a younger man Teddy might still be—someone who could stand up to those ambulance bullies and —but all poor Gracey could do was shake his wattles and try to get me to bed, oh—(*she laughs*) I don't mean—of course not—(*she stops*)—but I don't want to get him into trouble. Certainly not. He was very good to Teddy's ears. (*She drinks*) Oh, I do feel—feel—drinking by myself . . . Do excuse me, but it's been a bit of a—a bit of a . . .

Greaves Would you mind telling me how it happened, Mrs Treadley?

Molly What?

Eve You can't possibly ask her questions—you can see the state she's in. Now come, Molly, I insist . . .

Molly Oh, tush tush, Eve, tush, I'm perfectly all right, perfectly. And I want to—to help these men—now what was it you . . .?

Greaves How did it happen, Mrs Treadley?

Molly What?

Greaves How was Mr Treadley killed?

Eve Molly, don't . . .

Molly But it was an accident. Surely you know—haven't you told them, Evie, it was nobody's fault—except those men who were rough and poor old Gracey, it just—just happened you see, didn't it, Evie?

Greaves But Miss Mace wasn't in the room at the time.

Molly What? Oh—no, no, you weren't were you, darling, she generally comes in later, to clean up our messes for us, don't you, darling? (*She laughs*)

Greaves You and Mr Treadley were alone.
Molly What?
Greaves There was just you and Mr Treadley.
Molly Oh. Yes. Yes, that's right. Me and Mr—Teddy. And the cocktail cabinet, of course, that's always there, to make a third.
Eve Molly—(*she goes to her*)—don't talk now. Don't talk now.
Molly What, why, darling, there's nothing to be afraid of, is there?
Greaves No, Mrs Treadley.
Molly You see, it was just an accident. They understand that. That's all there is to it, isn't it?

Molly switches on the radio. Dance music plays

Greaves How did the accident happen?
Eve No. I won't permit this. You have no right to do this. Now, Molly...
Greaves Miss Mace! Mrs Treadley has offered to help us in our enquiries. If you persist in interrupting, I shall have to ask you to leave the room.
Molly What?
Greaves You were telling us what happened, Mrs Treadley.
Molly Well, it was—something ghastly happened, you see. He had an accident. I—I didn't really see it, my back must have been turned or I was looking away for a moment but—but then there he was. Spurting —spurting . . . Do you see?
Greaves One moment he was alive, and the next he was dying!
Molly Yes—well, he had these sudden changes of mood recently, didn't he, Evie? (*She laughs*) I'm sorry—I didn't mean . . . Oh, just a minute— (*she puts her glass down on the drinks trolley and picks up the gin bottle*)— need to—another little—a truth drink so you'll know I . . . (*She laughs and shows the bottle to Greaves*)
Eve No, Molly—no . . . (*She attempts to take the bottle from her*)

There is a short, absurd wrestle

Molly Bugger off, bitch!

Eve recoils

Sorry, Evie—sorry. Forgive please. Pretty please with sugar on it. (*She laughs, pours a drink, and turns grandly to Greaves*)

Eve This is dreadful, dreadful. I'm going to phone Dr Gracey and tell him . . .
Greaves That's your privilege, Miss.
Molly What, she's got a pash on me, haven't you, Evie . . .

Evie exits to the hall

(*sitting on the sofa*) Yes, she has, do you know about the pashes ladies have on ladies, ladies like her on ladies like me, are you married?
Greaves Yes.
Molly Is she pretty, your wife?

Greaves turns off the radio, closes the hall door and nods to the Constable, who takes out his notebook

Greaves You were going to tell me the truth, Mrs Treadley.
Molly What?
Greaves The truth.
Molly What about?
Greaves Your husband's death. (*He sits on the sofa*) He was murdered,
    wasn't he?
Molly Murdered? (*She yawns*) I'm sorry—sorry . . . what?
Greaves Did you do it?
Molly What?
Greaves You did, didn't you?
Molly What—what do you do to people, when you—you catch them?
Greaves That's for the courts to decide.
Molly But if they're children?
Greaves But there aren't any children, are there, Mrs Treadley?
Molly Oh yes. We're all children in this house, all of us. That's what
    caused it, you see. But nobody meant—oh please believe—it wasn't
    meant. He—he brought it on himself! He did! He did! An old man,
    come to the end, he wanted to die, he wanted to—full of hate—I
    couldn't bear his hate—and he knew—you see he knew—he was right,
    about his old man's smells, his deafness and the boredom, the boredom
    and the bellowing and the contempt and the pee-dribble and his pyjamas
    arsing—and—and . . .
Greaves And is that why you killed him, Mrs Treadley?
Molly What?
Greaves Did you kill him?
Molly I . . .

Pause

Eve enters from the hall

Eve I've spoken to Dr Gracey. He's coming over . . .
Molly (*rising and pointing at Eve*) It was her! She did it! She did it! (*Pause*)
    No, no, sorry, Evie, sorry, darling—it was me. Yes. I killed him. I killed
    him. I took the things and I—I . . . (*She makes thrusting movements,
    stops abruptly*) And now you all hate me, don't you—well, here I am,
    look at me, you—you—(*she throws out her arms for them to see her,
    then starts a slow move towards the Constable by the conservatory*)—
    what do you see, an old vamp, is that what you see, but you'd roger me,
    too, wouldn't you, I could make you love—I'm still—look—look . . .
    (*She starts to lift her nightdress to the Constable*)

*Greaves looks at Eve, who crosses quickly to Molly. Greaves rises. Eve grips
Molly by the shoulders and pulls her away, supporting her. Molly collapses
against Eve*

Bed now, Evie. Bed, please. Bed, darling . . .

The Lights fade to a BLACKOUT

SCENE 4

The same. Some months later. Afternoon

The room fills with light, steadily, to bright sunlight. There are dust sheets over the sofa, chairs and piano. On the sofa are Molly's scarf and handbag. The hall door is open

> *Eve enters from the corridor. She opens the french windows, removes the dust sheets from the piano and armchair, and folds them. She moves to the sofa, sees Molly's handbag, sits and starts to look through it. Molly enters from the hall, moves in and holds out her hand. Eve gives her the bag*

Molly Thank you, darling. I do wish people would stop rummaging through it, it's been emptied and refilled by so many different ladies recently, police ladies, prison ladies, hospital ladies, (*she takes out a cigarette*) it doesn't feel mine any more. (*She lights the cigarette*) What were you looking for, darling? The sleeping pills?

Eve I couldn't remember whether we'd brought them.

Molly Do we need them, though? Surely we don't mind being awake on an August afternoon? (*She takes a bottle out of her pocket*) Do you want to look after them?

Eve No, of course not, Moll.

Molly Oh, you might as well, darling. I'm not going to try again. For one thing, I don't seem to be very good at it, and I do hate the way they drag one back, with stomach pumps and sermons. Do take them, darling. There. (*She hands Eve the pills*)

Eve Well, if you . . . (*She takes the pills*) I'll make up a bed if you still want a lie down.

Molly Lie down?

Eve You said you had a headache.

Molly Did I? (*Wandering off to the conservatory*) Well then it's gone.

Eve Oh. Oh good! Well, what about our walk then?

Molly Our walk?

Eve You were looking forward to a walk.

Molly I think I'll leave it until tomorrow. To tell you the truth, darling, I'm a bit confused at finding everything so familiar.

Eve It's my fault. I shouldn't have agreed to let you come back—at least so soon.

Molly So soon? But I haven't been here for a long time. After such an eventful spring and a summer wasted in—in institutions—I'd have hated to have missed the old haunts in their autumn colours. I long to see them.

Eve You do want a walk then?

Molly What do you want, Evie?

Eve (*intensely*) I want our old Moll back again.

Molly Do you really? Our old judge found the old Moll a trifle too degenerate for his taste. Quite disgusting, in fact. Quite disgusting. Disgusting.

Eve He had no right—no right to say those things. They had no right to make you go through that trial, not after—after the truth had come out. I shall never believe in British justice again.

Molly Poor Eve! Still, think what we would have lost. The sight of old Treefe, for example, touching his forelock to thank everyone for all the trouble they were putting themselves to, to hang his son. Who's only just come of hangable age. (*Pause*) Can I have a drink? No—no more drinks for me.

Eve You must stop blaming yourself, Molly. You stood by him right to the bitter end.

Molly Not quite, darling. His bitter end comes on Monday week, at six in the morning, isn't it? He's going to that without me. (*Pause*) Did you notice how he kept looking across, as if he believed I could just come out of my box and into his, and cuddle him through it. His peaky face, and the spot blooming on his nose. Do you think he'll expect me on Monday week, too, right to the very last, as a child expects his mummy to come and take him away. (*She turns away*) I'd have made a good mother, wouldn't I?

Eve He did do it, Moll.

Molly Of course he did. (*Pause. She makes a violent gesture*) So hang the little beggar! By the way, darling, I haven't thanked you properly for bringing him to book. Thank you. If it hadn't been for you ...

Eve I couldn't let you sacrifice yourself. I couldn't, Moll.

Molly No. No, I don't suppose you could.

Eve We have to do right by those we care about.

Molly Yes. Yes we do. You love me, Evie, don't you?

Eve Yes.

Molly Thank you. (*She sits*)

Eve Oh Moll ... (*She gives a sudden shy smile*)

Molly It *is* a lovely afternoon, isn't it? Would you like a walk?

Eve I'd love one.

Molly Right. Off you go then.

They stare at each other

Darling, we really must start doing our separate wants, or how shall we live together? Please go, darling. (*Pause*) Please.

Eve exits through the conservatory

Molly sits staring ahead

Pretty please—(*pause*)—with sugar on it.

The Lights fade to a BLACKOUT, *as—*

the CURTAIN *falls*

FURNITURE AND PROPERTY LIST

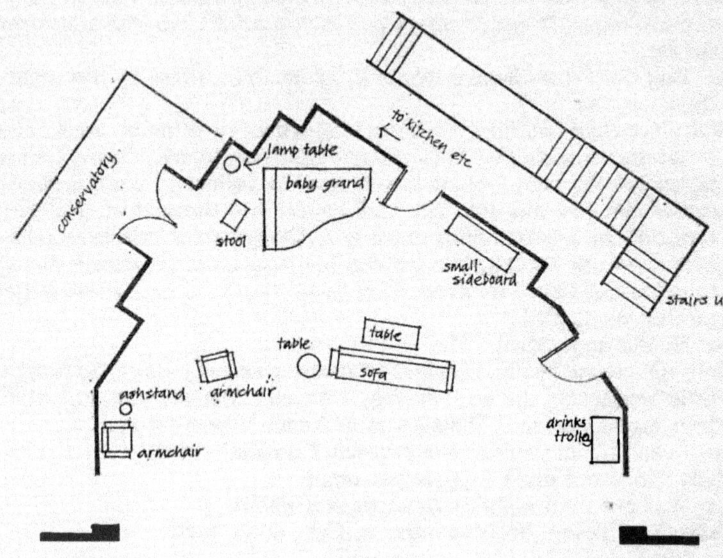

ACT I

Scene 1

On stage: Drinks trolley. *On it:* whisky, gin, sherry, assorted glasses, soda
    siphon, ashtray, other drinks as dressing, ice bucket, bottle opener
    Sofa. *On it:* cushions
    Sofa table. *On it:* magazines, ashtray. *Beside it:* wastepaper-basket
    Sideboard. *On it:* radio, dressing. *In drawer:* pencils, used papers,
    envelopes
    Occasional table by sofa. *On it:* ashtray
    2 armchairs. *Beside one:* ash-stand
    Piano. *On it:* sheet music
    Piano stool
    Occasional table by piano. *On it:* lamp
    Carpet
    Window curtains
    In conservatory: geraniums, pots, trays, gardening implements,
    including shears, dressing

Off stage: Oven gloves (**Eve**)
    Bottle of beer, mug (**Teddy**)

Personal: Eve: spectacles
    Teddy: hearing-aid, handkerchiefs
    Molly: scarf, gloves, handbag, cigarettes, lighter, matches

Scene 2

Strike:	Cigarette stub Beer bottle and top Mug Used glasses Cigarettes, matches
Set:	**Molly's** handbag on sofa with cigarettes, lighter and matches Piano open
Off stage:	Walking-stick **(Teddy)** **Teddy's** hat and coat **(Eve)**

Scene 3

Set:	Sofa cushions on floor Raincoat on sofa
Off stage:	Water to dampen clothing, etc. **(Eve, Teddy)**

ACT II

Scene 1

Strike:	All used glasses, cigarette butts, empty bottles Hearing-aid Raincoat and hat
Set:	Fresh gin, Scotch, clean glasses on drinks trolley. *On sofa:* **Eve's** knitting, **Molly's** handbag with cigarettes, lighter, matches, nose drops *On armchair back:* "blood" bag Tidy trolley Check garden shears in conservatory

Scene 2

Off stage:	Car keys **(Oliver)**

Scene 3

Strike:	Garden shears **Teddy's** armchair **Molly's** handbag, scarf, matches, cigarettes, lighter, sherry, whisky glass, other used glasses
Personal:	**Constable:** Notebook, pencil

Scene 4

Strike:	Gin, Scotch, used glasses
Set:	Dust sheets on sofa, piano, armchair **Molly's** handbag with matches, cigarettes, lighter on sofa
Personal:	**Molly:** bottle of pills

Special general note: As **Molly's** use of cigarettes is so important it is advisable to have standby cigarettes and matches on the drinks trolley and in other places where convenient, also off stage. Fresh packets should be set in the handbag whenever possible.

LIGHTING PLOT

Property fittings required: wall brackets, table lamp
Interior. A living-room. The same scene throughout

ACT I Scene 1   Afternoon
To open: General effect of late afternoon light

Cue 1   As CURTAIN rises   (Page 1)
Start very slow fade to dusk

Cue 2   **Molly, Teddy** and **Eve** exit   (Page 10)
Fade to BLACKOUT

ACT I Scene 2   Mid-afternoon
To open: General effect of afternoon light

Cue 3   **Molly:** ". . .over at Guilford?"   (Page 17)
Start slow fade to overcast, rainy light

Cue 4   **Oliver:** "Miss?" (2nd time)   (Page 21)
Fade to BLACKOUT

ACT II Scene 3   Late afternoon
To open: Effect of grey, wet afternoon light

Cue 5   **Eve:** "It's jolly well not fair!"   (Page 23)
Fade to BLACKOUT

ACT II Scene 1   Afternoon
To open: General effect of sunny afternoon

Cue 6   **Teddy:** "What?"   (Page 31)
Fade to BLACKOUT

ACT II Scene 2   Late afternoon
To open: General effect of afternoon light, two hours later

Cue 7   **Molly:** "Get help, you fool. Get help!"   (Page 35)
BLACKOUT

ACT II Scene 3 Evening
To open: Lamp and brackets on

Cue 8   **Molly:** "Bed, please. Bed, darling . . ."   (Page 39)
Fade to BLACKOUT

ACT II Scene 4   Afternoon
To open: Lights up steadily to bright sunlight

Cue 9   **Molly:** ". . . with sugar on it."   (Page 41)
Fade to BLACKOUT

EFFECTS PLOT

ACT I

SCENE 1

Cue 1	**Tedddy:** "Moll! Moll! Moll!" *Door slams upstairs*	(Page 1)
Cue 2	**Teddy:** ". . . hell's she playing at?" *Front doorbell rings*	(Page 3)

SCENE 2

Cue 3	**Molly** turns radio on *Music*	(Page 15)
Cue 4	**Molly** turns radio off *Music off*	(Page 15)
Cue 5	**Oliver:** "I can smell it—that's all" *Start rain effect, swell at end of scene, continue through change*	(Page 21)

SCENE 3

Cue 6	**Molly:** "Are you unhappy?" *Fade rain gradually*	(Page 21)
Cue 7	After **Oliver** exits *Door slams*	(Page 22)

ACT II

SCENE 1

Cue 8	**Eve:** ". . . couldn't hear what I heard" *Motor horn sounds*	(Page 25)
Cue 9	**Molly:** "Thank you. Thank you." *Thumping from upstairs, followed by motor horn*	(Page 29)

SCENE 2

No cues

SCENE 3

Cue 10	**Molly** turns radio on *Dance Music*	(Page 38)
Cue 11	**Greaves** turns radio off *Music off*	(Page 38)

www.ingramcontent.com/pod-product-compliance
Ingram Content Group UK Ltd.
Pitfield, Milton Keynes, MK11 3LW, UK
UKHW021822150726
7214IPUK00017B/267